AMAZON ECHO USER GUIDE: SUPPORT MADE EASY

RONALD PETER

Disclaimer

Copyright Notes

CONTENTS

ALL ABOUT THE AMAZON ECHO

The Amazon Echo is an Internet-connected speaker that can understand your voice and do things that you tell it to do.

Right now, you might be thinking to yourself, "So what? Doesn't Siri do the same thing?" or "I do all that through Google Voice already."

The difference between the Amazon Echo and every other similar product is that the Amazon Echo is always on and ready to serve you, and that makes a tremendous difference in the usability of the product. You can now have this functionality native in your home, and not tethered to a device.

Imagine you want to want some music to be played, or you want to stream Amazon Prime Music. No matter how you are set up at home, through your Sonos, through Spotify somehow, with a Roku on your TV, you have to follow the same sequence of steps. First, you find your tablet, remote, or laptop. Next, you open the application and filter through your gigantic library of music. Finally, once you have found the correct album or artist, you can hit play.

With the Amazon Echo, almost all the laborious steps are omitted. You don't need to connect your phone or tablet to a speaker system anymore, or wade through your music library. All you need to do is call out "Alexa, play

Desi Arnaz", and you can hear *Cuban Pete* being played in a couple of seconds in your living room.

Can't hear the music? Tell Alexa to pump up the volume. Too loud? Tell Alexa to get softer. You can hear the weather, change the music, or stop the music, all while you're doing dishes or watching your kids.

Imagine doing this for one day, then going into your car for the drive to work. Now you have to paw through a pile of CDs with your hands looking for the correct band, correct CD, and correct song you want to hear.

Instead of having a maid at home, we can now tell our furniture what to do. It's like we're the Jetsons!

The purpose of technology is to make our lives SIMPLER and save us TIME. If we spend $100 or $200 to make our lives more convenient, it's a great investment of money to get precious time back.

One extra benefit of the Amazon Echo is that it is also a Bluetooth speaker with excellent sound quality. The Echo has an unusually long range, assuming you are comparing it to a counter top CD player and not a shelf system. There is no subwoofer yet, however!

Merely playing music is only scratching the surface of what the Amazon Echo can do. You can ask it what song it is playing (you might not know what song it is if it is going through a playlist). It's faster to get the weather reports by asking your Echo than using any weather app. The Echo can also give you a summary of the news, from channels that you customize. Sports scores, traffic reports…the Echo is getting new features every month on a regular basis.

There's one more huge benefit that doesn't fit into the Echo playing audio back to you. The Echo can store a list for you. You can stuff up to 100 items into a shopping list.

The Echo can store a list for you.

I didn't know that some people were list-makers until I married my wife. There are papers all over the house, grocery lists, to-do lists, you name it. When we're cleaning the house, we find lists that she's made in the past and forgot that she made them. What we really need is a list that tells us where all the other lists are.

One hidden benefit of Amazon Echo's list-making ability is helping you declutter and clean up your life. It's easy to start making a list and forget about it, or leave the list at home when you're at the supermarket or at the mall.

For us, when we're doing housework or something happens that triggers a memory that we need to pick up something, we can call out to Alexa and have her add it to her list for us. It's the closest thing to an automated robot secretary that I've ever seen. The best part about it is you can't lose the list! It's stored in Amazon's cloud, and accessible through your computer app or your phone or tablet.

Now our supermarket list is never left at home, because it's always in our pocket. And if I'm at the store and my wife wants to add something to the list, she can have Alex add it and I will know about it right away. She no longer has to phone, email, or even text me…Amazon Echo will just make the right thing happen.

So there's a lot of fun stuff waiting to be explored with this new toy! I have heard from multiple spouses, both men and women, that the Amazon Echo is the only gadget they have purchased that their significant other has ever used. The difference with the Amazon Echo and other technological toys is that it is USEFUL!

I hope this book helps you get the most out of your new purchase!

SETTING UP THE AMAZON ECHO

The Amazon Echo, like a product from Apple, is packaged like a luxury piece of equipment. It does not have any batteries, so it will need to be installed close to a power supply. The dimensions of the Amazon Echo are 9 1/4 by 3 1/4 inches.

The Amazon Echo requires you to use the Echo app for installation, because there is no visual display on the Echo itself. The app can be used on your phone, tablet or computer.

To set up the Echo, you need an active wireless connection. The documentation from Amazon says:

- Amazon Echo connects to dual-band Wi-Fi (2.4Ghz / 5Ghz) networks that use the 802.11 a/b/g/n standard. It does not support enterprise or ad-hoc (or peer-to-peer) networks.
- From the Amazon Echo App, open the left navigation panel, and then select Settings > [NAME]'s Echo > Update Wi-Fi. If you're setting up Amazon Echo for the first time, or you're adding a new Amazon Echo to your account, select Set up a new Echo.
- On your Amazon Echo, press and hold the Action button for five seconds. The light ring changes to orange, and your mobile device connects to Amazon Echo. A list of available Wi-Fi networks appear in the app.

- Select your Wi-Fi network, enter the network password (if required), and then select Connect. If you don't see your Wi-Fi network, scroll down and select Add a Network or Rescan.

The Echo is designed to work in a HOME network environment. If you received it at work, and you try to connect it to the work wireless network, there are a few reasons why you may be unsuccessful. Some people have reported that they could not connect their Echo to their work network, but could connect it to their home network, and the difference was that their wireless Internet connection at work did not require a password. I believe the problem is listed in the Echo documentation: **Does not support enterprise or ad-hoc (or peer-to-peer) networks**. If you have the typical home wireless network secured with a single password, you should have no problems connecting the Echo.

The Amazon Echo requires a working wireless Internet connection to do just about everything - it needs Internet to speak, listen to you, and play music. If you have problems with your Echo, one of the first things to check is network connectivity. If other devices on your network can successfully connect to the Internet but your Echo cannot, an easy thing to test is moving the Echo closer to your router. If your Echo is typically located far away from your router, the signal can be weak and you can also get more interference from the wireless networks of your neighbors. Moving the Echo CLOSER to your router can eliminate two problems at once. If the Echo starts working again after you move it, you can try switching the wireless frequency, switching to the 5GHz band (this band has more frequencies available but a shorter range), or invest in a wireless signal booster.

Don't overlook the remote control. In the excitement of setting up the Echo and talking to a black cylinder, it is easy to forget that the remote exists. With the remote, you can extend the effective range of voice control over the Echo. There is a microphone in the remote. Not only can the remote listen just like Echo, it has some advantages. For example, you don't need to speak the wake words "Amazon" or "Alexa" when using the remote. The remote will also receive and process commands from your voice even if the Echo is muted.

Can My Echo Hear Me?

In the out-of-the box configuration, it can be difficult to tell if your Echo can hear you when you are giving it commands. Your in-laws may already suffer from selective hearing issues; you don't need a piece of technology giving you the same attitude! There is one setting you can change from the default that will let you know for sure if the Echo can hear your instructions or not. You make this change through the Echo app or the Echo web interface on your phone, tablet or computer. Under **Settings > [Your name]'s Echo > Sounds**, set **Wake up sound** to enabled.

Now, whenever you say "Alexa," you'll here a soft tone confirming she's awake and ready for your command.

In a similar vein, you can enable the **End of request** sound. This lets you know that the Echo is finished listening to you, and will start processing your command.

Non-US Echo Users

Although the only OFFICIAL way to get an Amazon Echo is to go through the waitlist process, there is a brisk Echo market on Ebay and other third-party websites. If you have an Amazon Echo and you don't live in America, you will have to do a little more work to use all the features Echo provides, or some things may not work at all.

The main issue is Amazon Echo is designed to work with US postal codes. The Echo will not recognize non-US zip codes. If you live in Canada or Mexico, you can at least pick a US zip code that will put you in the time zone. You can enter in a US postal code that is close to where you are. Unfortunately, you may live in an area that does not recognize daylight savings time, but the location you pick in the US does recognize daylight savings time (only Arizona does not).

If you change the zip code to make the time correct, the local weather report will be broken, because the Echo will think you are in a different location. You have to choose between having the time correct, or having the weather correct. And this is just for people who live in the same general area as the United States - if you are in a country a great distance from America, you won't be able to get either time or the weather correct.

Amazon claims that international weather reports are available, but in our experience it sometimes has difficulty locating smaller international cities.

GETTING AMAZON TO CHANGE YOUR SHIP DATE

Just getting an invitation to buy an Echo is an ordeal in itself, but once you get the invitation and try to buy one, many of us were dismayed that the wait time was four to six months.

If you're lucky, there is a way to speed up the wait time by a few months.

On the Amazon web site, under "Your Account", there is a section for Open Orders. If you're like most of us, the only open order you have is for an Amazon Echo several months from now.

To (hopefully) speed up the process, what you want to do is click **Change shipping speed**. On the next screen, you can select FREE standard shipping, FREE super saver shipping, or $5.99 one day shipping.

Keep the shipping speed the same (whatever it was before you came to this screen), and click "Confirm". The shipping speed won't change, but if there are earlier slots available for the Echo, your shipment date will change in a good way.

No one is sure exactly why this works, and your mileage may vary, of course. There have been reports of people clicking "Confirm" every day, seeing their shipment date move up, then seeing their shipment date move back again. This trick is most useful to someone who placed an Amazon Echo order about a month ago, and is desparate for a shipping speed increase. It's not recommended if your Echo is coming in a few weeks or a couple of months.

GAMES, INFORMATION AND OTHER FUN THINGS TO ASK

At launch, Amazon Echo was limited to passively responding to instructions from the owner. This worked well if you just wanted a maid or domestic servant, but what customers quickly asked for was a responsive interaction with the Echo. Amazon is constantly adding new features to the Echo through software updates.

Games

- **Simon Says**: Remember the childhood game of Simon Says? By saying "Alexa, Simon says" and then a phrase, your Echo will repeat whatever you say next in her female voice. The voice recognition is extremely accurate, unless you ask her to repeat a phrase that has pre-censored words in it. In that case, Alexa will bleep out parts of a word or a phrase that she is too modest to repeat. Light cussing (e.g., "crap") will make it through the filter. More vigorous expletives are still repeated, but a bleep may cover part of the offending word. You can covertly use the remote control from another room to get Echo to repeat what you say and surprise your family. These are all fun trivial games now, but you can imagine scenarios where this functionality is useful instead of a game. With a remote in a large house, the Echo can effectively function as an intercom through Simon says. If you have the remote in your pocket, you can always call for help if you get hurt in the garage or doing yard work outside.

- **Flip a Coin**: Can't decide where to eat? Perhaps the children can't decide which parent they love more. Solve these problems by asking, "Alexa, flip a coin."
- **Rock, Paper, Scissors**: If you need to decide a winner in an unambiguous and indisputable way, you can settle it with "Alexa, rock, paper, scissors."

Information

The number one requested addition to Echo's information was traffic reports. Traffic information is limited to a daily commute, and probably limited to the United States. A starting address and ending address are entered into Echo through the app. By default, the starting address is tie address the Echo is registered to. Once Echo has been configured correctly, you can ask Echo some information about your commute. You may want Echo to suggest a route for you to take, or get an estimated travel time.

You can ask Echo these questions about your commute:

- Alexa, how is traffic?
- Alexa, what's my commute?
- Alexa, what's traffic like right now?

More detailed information, such as alternate routes and travel times, is visible on the Echo app. The traffic information comes from Nokia.

Amazon Echo can tell you some factual information about your favorite sports teams. Supported sports are the NBA and NHL, with other American sports to come. For example, you can say, "Alexa, who won the Los Angeles Lakers game?" or "Alexa, when do the San Jose Sharks play next?" Supported questions are the results of the last game played by the team and the time and date of the next game that will be plated by the team.

Scores and Schedules-We heard your feedback that you'd like sports scores and schedules, and we wanted to let you know that Echo can now tell you the results of your favorite team's last game as well as the time and date of its next one. To give it a try, simply say, "Alexa, who won the Chicago Bulls game?" or "Alexa, when do the Detroit Red Wings play next?" Echo supports the NBA and NHL-with the NFL, MLB, MLS, NCAA basketball, and others soon to follow!

You can ask Echo the weather forecast for specific cities in America. For example, "Alexa, what's the weather in Orlando this weekend?"

If you ask Echo a factual question, she sometimes knows the answer and sometimes she doesn't; it's pretty hit and miss. The most basic factual questions are usually handled well, such as dates of major events, capital cities, and birthdays of major historical figures. Questions that are slightly less well known may or may not have an answer. For example, if you ask who a specific president's vice president was, you don't always get an answer (Yes for George W. Bush, no for George H.W. Bush, yes for Eisenhower, no for Cleveland, etc.). Echo can tell you a brief (2 sentence) description of the French Revolution and its dates, but not a description of Robespierre.

If Echo doesn't understand your question, she will send the question through a Bing search to your Echo app. If she doesn't understand your statement, she will tell you it doesn't understand.

Other Fun Things To Ask

Alexa, all your base are belong to us.
Alexa, are you sleepy?
Alexa, beam me up!
Alexa, do you like green eggs and ham?
Alexa, do you think I'm pretty?
Alexa, how are babies made?
Alexa, how much is that doggie in the window?
Alexa, how much wood can a woodchuck chuck?
Alexa, I am your father.
Alexa, I want the truth.
Alexa, is there a Santa?
Alexa, it's my birthday!
Alexa, live long and prosper.
Alexa, make me a sandwich.
Alexa, may the Force be with you!
Alexa, my name is Inigo Montoya.

Alexa, one fish, two fish.
Alexa, party on, Wayne!
Alexa, Romeo, Romeo, wherefore art thou Romeo?
Alexa, show me the money!
Alexa, surely, you can't be serious.
Alexa, tea. Earl Grey. Hot.
Alexa, tell me a St. Patrick's Day joke.
Alexa, what are you wearing?
Alexa, what do you like?
Alexa, what do you think about Cortana?
Alexa, what do you think about Google Now?
Alexa, what do you think about Siri?
Alexa, what does the earth weigh?
Alexa, what is the airspeed velocity of a swallow?
Alexa, what is the best tablet?
Alexa, what is the meaning of life?
Alexa, what is your favorite color?
Alexa, what is your quest?
Alexa, what was the Lorax?
Alexa, when is the end of the world?
Alexa, where am I?
Alexa, where do you live?
Alexa, Wikipedia [SUBJECT]
Alexa, who's your daddy?
Alexa, who shot first?
Alexa, why do you sit there like that?
Alexa, you're so cool!

PLAYING MUSIC AND PODCASTS

Amazon Echo plays music in your Prime Library the easiest, then music from TuneIn and iHeartRadio is slightly more complicated. There is minor support for Spotify, iTunes, and Pandora.

If you ask the Echo to play music, it will look in your Music Library (not all the songs available through Prime) first, and if finds a successful match, it will stop looking and play the song or artist. For example, "Alex, play the Rolling Stones" will play Rolling Stones songs in your library, and nothing else.

If there are more Rolling Stones songs available in Prime that you don't have in your library, Echo won't look outside the library for these songs. To force Echo to look in Prime for music, you can add that criteria to your command. "Alexa, play the Rolling Stones in Prime" will make Echo query the available music in Amazon Prime music first, and play the songs by that artist (if any) that are in prime.

When a song is playing on Amazon Echo, you can use your voice as a remote to control the Echo. "Rewind" will restart the song/music. "Pause" and "Continue" work just as the words describe. So does "Skip".

The Echo is very good at voice recognition, but it doesn't work correctly all the time. If it can't figure out what you're saying, you can ask Echo all day long and just won't work. Here's one email about this problem that came into us:

Currently Amazon Prime stations do not work with Amazon Echo, but they do work with iHeart radio.

Ron, I uploaded some dramatized stories to my library and put them into a playlist called Drama. I kept asking Alexa to play the Drama playlist and she kept saying she couldn't find it. I tried all sorts of things and nothing seemed to make it work. Do you have any advice?

This was quite a problem until I suggested to the user that she try asking the Echo how to spell Drama. Echo gave her the spelling, and after the spelling confirmation, Echo was able to find the playlist.

Now, I'm not sure WHY that worked. We checked the app before to make sure Echo knew the word drama correctly, and Echo understood it. Her Echo can find the drama playlist just fine now. In the absence of further support from Amazon, this is one approach that is worth trying when it can't understand a playlist.

Podcasts

Amazon Echo has some support for podcasts. For some people, this will be more useful than any music playing, but there is one huge gotcha.

The problem is that the Echo can only play the latest episode of a podcast.

I have tried "Alexa, play Flash TV Talk podcast episode 3" and "Alexa, Play Flash TV Talk podcast episode Listener Call-In Show" and every variation I can think of. The Echo invariably does the same thing, which is "I'm playing the latest episode of the Flash TV Talk podcast." If I am listening to Dan Carlin's Hardcore History podcast about the death of the Roman Republic and I have listened up to Death Throes of the Republic I, I cannot very well just skip to Death Throes of the Republic V without interrupting my listening experience.

This missing functionality makes the podcast feature, which is one feature I am quite interested in, not live up to its full potential. The "latest episode" of any given podcast is rarely what I want to listen to. Listening to Freakonomics or Stuff You Should Know will work well if I remember to listen every week, but even when I try to listen to every episode I end up skipping several and then listening to a 3 to 5 episode marathon, which you cannot do with the Echo.

If you listen to a podcast that is not episodic, this limitation may not affect you too much. Perhaps you listen to "This American Life" occasionally, and playing only the latest podcast will be fine to you as long as it is an episode that you haven't heard before.

For serious podcast listeners, Echo needs to add a specific episode search, as well as a way to remember the last episode of the podcast you have listened to. This way, you can automatically play the next podcast in line without having to pull out your phone and manually make Echo play an episode or look up where you are in a podcast series. The future is saying, "Alexa, play the next episode of Revolutions podcast."

Other Music Services: TuneIn, iHeartRadio, Spotify, iTunes, and Pandora

If you want to play music through the Echo directly and you don't want to use the Amazon Music Library, your choices are TuneIn and iHeartRadio. To use all the features of iHeartRadio, you will have to create a free iHeart Radio account and link it to your Amazon Echo. Among other things, the account is required to create custom radio stations based on an artist. If you are still waiting for your Echo to arrive, you can set up your iHeartRadio account while you are waiting.

Only a few other music services are supported at all by the Echo, and they require a second device to play the music and communicate with the Echo over Bluetooth. The addition of Spotify, iTunes, and Pandora came after the Echo's launch, so it is possible there will be a more complete integration of these music services directly into Echo in the future. We know it is technically possible to stream Pandora directly to the Echo, so the only questions are if Amazon wants to provide this functionality to Echo users.

To use this feature, first pair your phone or tablet with Echo by saying "Alexa, pair my device." After your music begins playing, you can control the playback of your music service by saying the wake word and: play, pause, stop, next, or previous.

Bluetooth

To activate Bluetooth connectivity, say "Alexa, pair my device." This will start the process of configuring Echo to act as a Bluetooth speaker. In this setup, all audio from a paired Bluetooth device will be redirected to Echo.

The most common way you would use this functionality is to play music from your phone. Echo has no storage space, so you can't load and store a song directly on the Echo. To play music, it has to have a music source. This source can be a paired phone, or it can be streaming over the internet.

Even if you have Echo set up as a Bluetooth speaker for your phone, voice calls must still be answered with and completed by the phone.

If you think about the Echo as an Internet connected Bluetooth speaker with a radio connection, the device truly shows its value. A Bluetooth speaker with these features could easily $200 by itself, but there is more to the Echo than this. You can use voice commands with this speaker and ask it questions.

OTHER FUNCTIONALITY

The Amazon Echo can perform a few functions outside of music and games out of the box.

Lists

It supports two different types of lists. The first list is a shopping list. For people who are afraid of big brother, it seems like this is the first step in having Amazon make a list of all the things you need, then you clicking a button and having Amazon DELIVER all the stuff you need. For now, it is simply a convenient way to create a list, then you can choose how to fulfill the items on your list by yourself.

At launch, you could create your shopping lists on Echo, but you could only see the shopping list through the app or on your computer. After a recent update, the Echo is now capable of reciting back items on your shopping list. Instruct Alexa to read your shopping list by saying, "Alexa, what's on my shopping list?"

Amazon Echo also has a to-do list, but it is not as effective as the shopping list because a to-do list is inherently more complicated. It's a little difficult to set up due dates and learning the correct phrasing of a request to get Alexa to understand what you are telling her. As a result, the to-do list is imprecise and finicky, and using it feels a little clumsy.

Alarms and Timers

You can set an alarm or a countdown timer in Amazon Echo. The alarm cannot be scheduled to repeat and only works if your desired alarm time is within the next 24 hours. Because there is no scheduling, this feature is less useful for someone using it as a daily alarm, but if you are timing an activity in the house, it is convenient because you don't need to march over to a clock; you can just call out to Alexa and create a new alarm or countdown.

Voice Training

Amazon Echo has a explicit voice training exercise which will help the device respond more accurately to your voice. The exercise consists of you saying 25 different phrases. After you have spoken these phrases normally into Amazon Echo (without shouting), she should be more responsive to you within a few minutes.

There is also an implicit voice training that is always going on without you actively participating. When you use the wake word to talk to Amazon Echo, the audio stream includes a few seconds of audio before the wake word, and stops once Amazon Echo has processed your question or request. These recordings are accessible if you log into Amazon's browser-based dashboard. Interactions are grouped by question or request. You can listen to your audio clip and send feedback about how well it was processed.

For the privacy conscious, individual clips can be deleted, or the entire history wiped out. Removing the recordings will negatively affect Echo's accuracy will take a dive back to out-of-the-box condition if you do so.

Flash Briefing

The flash briefing is a daily news report that is completely customizable depending on the types of news you want to listen to. Currently, it can only pull from a preselected list of Amazon news sources and tell you weather updates, but hopefully in future updates you will be able to pick your own sources of news and really have your favorite news from your constant companion.

USING THE APP

The companion App for Echo adds one thing that would be a really nice addition to Echo out of the box, but would add a lot to the cost: a screen. This functionality lets Echo communicate back to you without using words.

The screen is nice if you have a lot of information you want to pull out of Echo (a long shopping list) or you want to do complicated manipulation. Telling Alexa to play a song is easy, but telling Alexa to create a playlist or add to your library is complicated.

From the app, you can see what song is currently playing on the Echo and her queue of music. You can tap on an item to jump directly to that song, or add songs to your Music Library from a queue of Amazon Prime music.

If you can't find your phone, you can use http://echo.amazon.com to manipulate echo through your web browser. This will also let you PRINT OUT your shopping list.

If your tablet or phone loses connection with your Echo, you can delete the app, reinstall the app, and everything will be synced together.

TROUBLESHOOTING

The Echo is a new piece of technology, but we only have two old troubleshooting tips.

Reset the Unit

If the Echo freezes, or stops listening to your commands, or can't process your commands anymore, the first thing to try is a soft reset. At the bottom of the Echo is a hole you can insert a paper clip into. If you reset the Echo, sometimes your problem will be fixed right away.

Unplug the Unit Overnight

If the paper clip trick doesn't work, there's one more thing you can try. One person wrote in to us with this problem:

My Amazon Echo took a fall a couple of days ago. I bumped the table that it is normally on. It fell over, rolled over the edge, and crashed three feet, hitting the hard floor. The cord fell out during the fall. I plugged it back in and it seemed OK. About five minutes later, it started playing music without being told. I said, "Alexa, stop!" which worked, but the music started playing again a few minutes later, and the volume kept changing on its own.

I unplugged it and left it for a while, then plugged it back in but the same problems were happening. I must have unplugged and replugged five or six times but nothing seemed to work. Alexa still listened to my commands, but she played music whenever she wanted to.

For this woman, unplugging the Echo OVERNIGHT, then plugging it in again in the morning reset her Echo.

This is one more troubleshooting step you can take on your own; make sure you wait overnight or a full 12 hours, don't get impatient!

EPILOGUE

If this book was helpful to you, please leave a review of this book on Amazon! Every review helps!

For the latest Amazon Echo-related news, please sign up for updates! It's easiest to keep you informed via email!

Sign up for updates by going to:
http://www.toppingspublishing.com/amazonecho/

OTHER BOOKS BY RONALD PETER

KINDLE UNLIMITED: A GUIDE FOR YOUR QUESTIONS AND INFORMATION FOR YOU

Kindle Unlimited is Amazon's 'all-you-can-eat' subscription offering for books. We receive plenty of questions about Kindle Unlimited. We sorted through all the questions, organized them, and present the answers to your questions in a readable way. You'll also learn one little-known secret about Kindle ebooks!

AMAZON PRIME AND KINDLE LENDING LIBRARY: ALL THE BENEFITS OF YOUR AMAZON PRIME SUBSCRIPTION

The big draw of Amazon Prime is the shipping benefits, which are worth the price of admission. There's a lot more to Prime than shipping, and Amazon keeps adding new things every few months.

Learn how to watch movies on Amazon Prime. Called Amazon Prime Instant Video, this service lets you watch free videos on your computer, phone or tablet. These movies and television shows are already included with your Amazon Prime subscription, and once again, they're FREE!

Amazon doesn't promote this feature, but you are able to share your shipping benefits with up to four family members. This is just one of the little-known features of Amazon Prime!

The Kindle Owner's Lending Library lets you borrow one book per month, as long as you own a Kindle or a Fire Phone. If you didn't know about this feature, or could never get it to work, we have clear step-by-step instructions on how to get your monthly free download. Learn how to browse the Kindle store lending library for your free books! We also include information on Amazon's newest offerings, Prime Pantry and Amazon Elements! Everything is clearly explained in easy steps so you can use all the features of your Amazon Prime subscription like a pro.

AN EXERPT FROM AMAZON PRIME AND KINDLE LENDING LIBRARY: ALL THE BENEFITS OF YOUR AMAZON PRIME SUBSCRIPTION

The Amazon Music Library is populated in different ways. You can think of it like a digital cloud storage locker that you upload your songs to. Once the songs are in your Music Library, they can be listened to on whatever device (phone, tablet, computer) that can run the Amazon Music app.

In 2013 Amazon announced AutoRip. AutoRip simultaneously added an MP3 copy of each song on a CD to your Music Library whenever you bought a CD. Even better, Amazon went back in time, looked at your music purchase history since 1998, and added MP3 copies of each of THOSE songs to your Music Library. You may have not known Amazon Music Library existed before this moment, but your Music Library has always been there in the cloud, waiting for you to listen to it.

To summarize, your Music Library (before we introduce Prime Music) is a combination of songs you actively decide to put in the Music Library, and songs that are passively added by Amazon when you purchase a CD.

Prime Music lets you add songs Amazon has managed to license for streaming to your Music Library. Prime Music has a patchwork selection of artists and songs. Several major artist are simply missing from the catalog, and if an artist is included, some albums are included and others may not be. Even if an album is included in Prime Music, some tracks of the album may be left out.

Prime Music is limited by design to songs that are at least six months old; you always have to pay for newly released music.

Remember, when you're browsing Prime Music from a web browser, what you're doing is adding songs from Prime Music into your own personal Music Library. To play the music, you go to your Music Libary, where you can see all the songs that you have purchased from Amazon or songs you have uploaded yourself.

In the music player, you can shuffle songs within an individual playlist or songs within an album, but you cannot shuffle all your Prime Music at once. You are only authorized to listen to Prime Music on one device at a time, so if you are using your Amazon Fire TV Stick you cannot simultaneously listen on your phone.

For some songs, lyrics will be available and displayed while the music is playing. Songs that have lyrics available are labeled "Lyrics" next to the song title. Lyrics are timed to the song playback and displayed line by line. Lyrics may be available for songs that have been added to your Music Library through the digital music store or songs that have been uploaded by you to your Music Library and automatically matched by Amazon to a song in the digital music store catalog.

The apps for Prime Music are more streamlined than the web browser experience. The Amazon Prime libraries and your personal music libraries are merged, so you don't have the jarring experience of going back and forth from Prime Music to your Music Library.

Fire TV Stick User Guide: Support Made Easy

The Amazon Fire TV Stick is designed to be easy to set up, but let's make sure you're getting the most out of your purchase. You'll learn how to watch movies through Amazon Prime, how to watch movies in your own preexisting movie collection, viewing photos, listening to music, installing official apps, and sideloading apps.

TV Without Cable: Guide to Free Internet TV and Over-the-Air Free TV

Tired of Comcast, Dish, or DirectTV?

We're on hold with them for hours, and if we're lucky enough to get a representative who speaks English, they schedule an appointment two weeks in the future. Why does paying for cable services cost over $100/month?

Wondering What the Best Setup Is For Home?

Every day new services or devices are announced, each one promising to make our lives better and simpler. They all sound the same - do you want to have a detailed comparison and recommended setups for your living room TV?

In this book, we'll talk about ways you can watch the shows you want to watch, whenever you want to watch them. Movies, television, and sports!

CHROMECAST SETUP: SUPPORT AND USER GUIDE

Learn about all the different ways of casting and how to connect Chromecast to TVs in difficult situations, from hotel rooms to airports. Buy this book today on Amazon!

Made in the USA
Monee, IL
05 November 2026

68030309R10023